GREEK ISLAND MYTHS

DELOS
BIRTHPLACE OF APOLLO

JILL DUDLEY

PUT IT IN YOUR POCKET SERIES
ORPINGTON PUBLISHERS

Published by
Orpington Publishers

Cover design and origination by
Creeds, Bridport, Dorset
01308 423411

Printed and bound in the UK by
Creeds

© Jill Dudley 2017

ISBN: 978-0-9934890-6-8

DELOS

BIRTHPLACE OF APOLLO

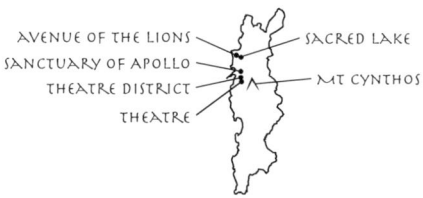

It is the light that first strikes the visitor to Delos. On arrival at this tiny island at the centre of the Cyclades, a pure bright lustre reflects off the mushroom grey of the island with its white marble ruins. Maybe it was this island of his birth that gave Apollo the epithet Phoebus – Phoebus Apollo, Apollo the shining one.

According to legend, Apollo's mother Leto, an immortal Titaness, was loved by Zeus, supreme god of the heavens and the Olympians, and she became pregnant with twins by him. When Hera, wife of Zeus, learned of it she was furious and forbade the earth to allow Leto to give birth anywhere under the sun. Leto wandered far and wide searching for a place willing to receive her for her confinement, and risk Hera's wrath. Lord Zeus eventually requested help from his brother

Poseidon, god of the sea.

Poseidon told Zeus of this small island which until then had been submerged and drifting aimlessly, an island known as *A-delos,* meaning 'invisible'. In response to the call for assistance, Poseidon brought the island to the surface and secured it on four columns of diamonds. *A-delos* now became Delos – the word means 'visible', 'manifest'.

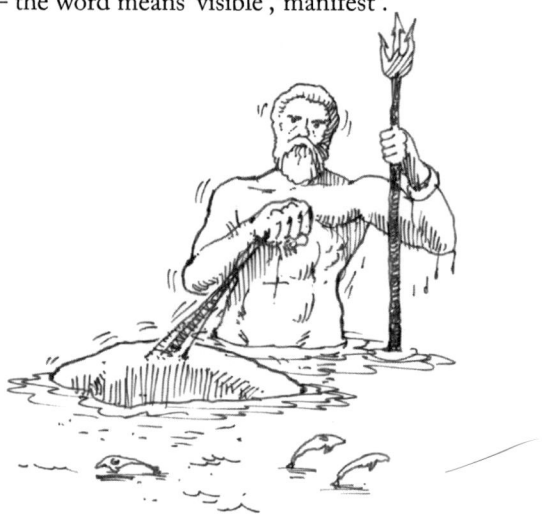

The tiny island, however, was afraid that Hera would take revenge and kick her back under the sea. It was not until Leto swore an oath on the river Styx (the greatest oath possible to be taken by an immortal) that the god to be born would build a temple on her soil and, in consequence, she would become the most revered island in the Hellenic world, that Delos agreed to allow the birth to take place there.

Leto's promise to make Delos famous throughout the world was kept, and for centuries this small island was a centre of pilgrimage. Even today boatloads of enthusiasts come daily throughout the summer so that the authorities ration visitors to a few hours only on the island.

From the ancient port a track can be taken to a solitary palm tree which is visible from the sea. It marks the spot where Apollo was born. To reach it the Terrace of the Lions is passed, large sculpted marble beasts squatting on their haunches, their front legs upright, and facing east towards the Sacred Lake and rising sun. The lake is now dry but, at the time of Apollo's birth, it was fed by the river Inopeus which flowed down Mt. Cynthos, a low mountain in the centre of the island.

Leto's confinement lasted nine days and, as her birth pangs increased, she clung to the trunk of the palm tree. Several goddesses attended her but Hera, continuing her fit of jealousy, kept Eileithyia, goddess of childbirth, hidden in a cloud on Mt. Olympus.

Eventually Iris, goddess of the rainbow, was sent to fetch Eileithyia with a bribe of a gold necklace, and they managed to escape from Hera and arrive on Delos in time to help with the immortal birth.

According to Homer's *Hymn to Apollo*, when Apollo was born ...*all Delos blossomed with gold, as when a hill-top is heavy with woodland flowers, beholding the child of Zeus and Leto...* The infant Apollo was wrapped in swaddling clothes edged with gold and fed nectar and ambrosia, the food of the gods. But the swaddling clothes could not contain Apollo and he burst forth from them crying *'May the harp and the bending bow be my delight, and I shall prophesy to men the unerring will of Zeus.'*

In the far north-east of the island are the Stadium and Gymnasium where the Delia was held, said to have been a festival founded by Theseus after he had killed the Minotaur on Crete*. The festival was held every four years, a celebratory gathering from many islands to worship Apollo with events such as gymnastics, musical contests, choruses and dances.

After Theseus' success on Crete he ran away to the island of Naxos* with Ariadne, King Minos' daughter, where they lived happily until Dionysos, god of wine and drama, ordered Theseus in a dream to leave the island because he himself had designs on Ariadne. On his way back to Athens it is said that Theseus called in at Delos to offer up sacrifice to Apollo. He brought with him a small wooden statue of Aphrodite, goddess of love, a statue which Ariadne had given him. This statue Theseus dedicated to Apollo, either because he no longer cared for Ariadne or, as the kindly second century A.D. travel-writer Pausanius wrote, because he could not bear to be reminded constantly of his love for her. In all events, Theseus finally married an Amazon queen by whom he had a son, then married Ariadne's sister, Phaedra, who fell in love with her step-son, and everybody died unhappily in typical Greek-tragedy fashion.

To get to Mt Cynthos, the highest point on Delos, the visitor has to pass through a maze of ruined houses, shops and temples. There are several sanctuaries in honour of Egyptian gods from the time of Alexander the Great in the fourth century B.C., a temple of Isis, for example, and another of Serapis. There is also a temple of Hera which is surprising, considering her anger at her husband Zeus fathering Apollo; but, no doubt, the temple was built to appease and honour her as a goddess of women and marriage.

When Theseus set off from Athens to Crete as one of the victims to be fed to the Minotaur, his intention had been to kill the monster and put an end to this annual tribute which King Minos of Crete had been exacting from Athens for the death of his son. The Athenians made a vow that if Theseus was successful they would send a sacred embassy to Delos every year to give thanks to Apollo. While the ship from Athens was gone no execution of any Athenian prisoner was allowed until the ship's return. This was why Socrates, when condemned to die for allegedly corrupting the minds of young men regarding the gods, had a stay of execution till the boat had returned from Delos.

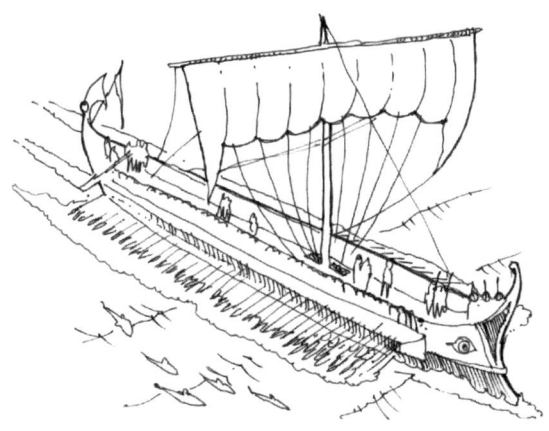

Coming back down from Mt. Cynthos the visitor sees another labyrinth of ruined houses – the House of the Masks, the House of Dolphins and the House of Dionysos, each one with fine mosaic floors. There is also a large theatre facing west towards the Bay of Fourni and the Delos Straits.

From the theatre it is easy to imagine the *trireme* arriving on its annual mission from Athens and docking in the ancient port. On its arrival, those sent on the embassy would go in procession to the temple of Apollo singing a hymn recounting the story of Leto and the birth of Apollo and his divine sister, Artemis, goddess of hunting. They intoned chants in honour of Apollo while making a solemn tour of the sanctuary of the god. Afterwards they would sacrifice to Apollo and the games consisting of athletics, horse-racing, and musical contests would begin. The *Geranos,* or sacred Crane dance, a dance with serpentine movements introduced by Theseus representing the labyrinth from which he had emerged from the Minotaur's lair, would be performed.

Nearly all that remains of Apollo's temple today is the Propylaea, the ceremonial gateway, which consists of three well-worn marble steps with Doric columns. But the stories of Apollo live on – Phoebus Apollo, Apollo the shining one, a god of light. As the visitor sails away again, the lustre and sparkle of this island (this solitaire diamond) remains indelibly stamped on the mind, never to be forgotten. It is quite possible that the memory is enhanced by dolphins (sacred to Apollo) playing around the boat, arching out and plunging back into the sea.

* Denotes a separate booklet on the subject.

SOME GODS BORN OF ZEUS

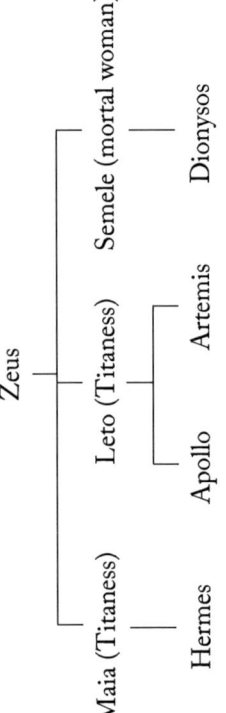

FAMILY TREE OF THE TITANS, GODS AND GODDESSES

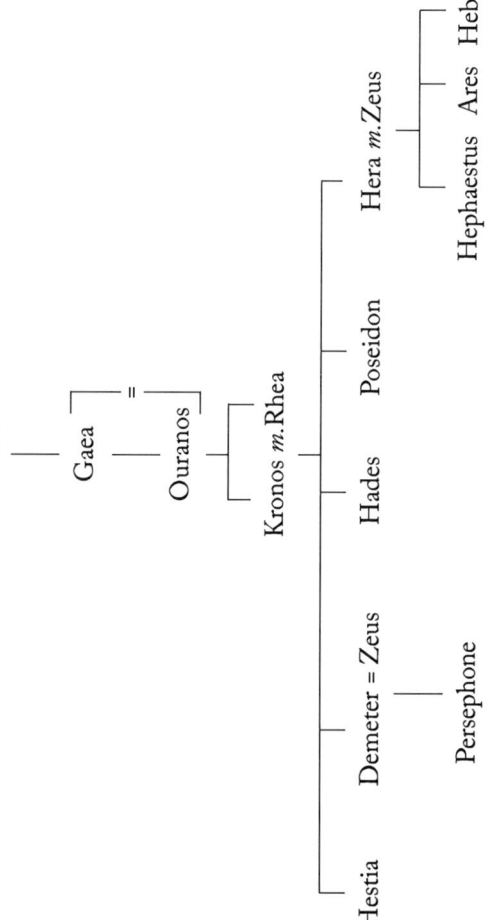

GLOSSARY OF GODS

APHRODITE – Goddess of love. There are two stories of her birth. One that she was the daughter of Zeus and Dione, the other that she arose fully grown from the sea at Paphos in Cyprus. She was married to the lame god Hephaestus.

APOLLO – Son of Zeus and the Titaness Leto. He was twin brother of Artemis, and god of medicine, music, archery and prophecy.

ARTEMIS – Twin sister of Apollo. Although she was goddess of hunting, she was also protectress of wild life and defender of the very young.

DIONYSOS – Son of Zeus and the mortal woman Semele. He was god of wine and drama.

EILEITHYIA – Goddess of childbirth.

HERA – Wife and sister of Zeus. She was goddess of women and marriage.

IRIS – Goddess of the rainbow.

ISIS – A great Egyptian goddess. She was wife of Osiris and mother of Horus.

LETO – A Titaness, and mother of Apollo and Artemis by Zeus.

MINOS – Son of Zeus and Europa, daughter of the King of Tyre. Minos became king of Crete.

MINOTAUR – Half-man, half-bull, and offspring of Pasiphae, wife of King Minos of Crete. Due to Poseidon's anger with King Minos for keeping a bull he had sent him to be sacrificed to him, he punished him by causing Pasiphae to fall in love with the animal.

POSEIDON – Brother of Zeus and Hera. He was god of the sea as well as of earthquakes and horses.

SERAPIS – A late god introduced into Egyptian worship by Ptolemy I after the death of Alexander the Great, in order to unite Egyptians and Greeks in a common worship.

TITANS – The offspring of Ouranos (often spelt Uranus, the heavens) and Gaea (the earth). There were said to be twelve of them, six sons and six daughters. Kronos was one of the sons, and Rhea one of the daughters. These two gave birth to Poseidon, Hera, Zeus and several other of the Olympian gods.

ZEUS – Son of Kronos and Rhea, and husband of Hera. He was god of the heavens, and supreme god of the ancient world having deposed his father.

MORE FROM THE PUT IT IN YOUR POCKET SERIES

TROJAN WAR
THE JUDGEMENT OF PARIS
HELEN
KING AGAMEMNON
ACHILLES
THE WOODEN HORSE
ODYSSEUS

SACRED SITES
ATHENS – THE ACROPOLIS
CORINTH – ST. PAUL AND THE GODDESS OF LOVE
DELPHI – THE ORACLE OF APOLLO
ELEUSIS – DEMETER AND KORE
EPIDAURUS – CENTRE OF HEALING
OLYMPIA – THE OLYMPIC GAMES

ALSO BY JILL DUDLEY

YE GODS! (TRAVELS IN GREECE)

YE GODS! II (MORE TRAVELS IN GREECE)

LAP OF THE GODS (TRAVELS IN CRETE AND THE AEGEAN ISLANDS)